Jamila Gavin

Other authors in
the series:

Theresa Breslin, Gillian Cross,
Michelle Magorian, Michael Morpurgo,
Jenny Nimmo, Anne Fine, J.K. Rowling,
Jacqueline Wilson

Joanna Carey is an author and illustrator in
her own right. She is a former children's books
editor of *The Guardian*, and still contributes.
She is also a regular reviewer for the
Times Educational Supplement.
Joanna also interviewed Jacqueline Wilson
and Michael Morpurgo for this series.

First published in Great Britain 2002 by Egmont Books Limited,
239 Kensington High Street, London W8 6SA.

Interview questions, design and typesetting © 2002
Egmont Books Limited
Interview answers © 2002 Jamila Gavin
Jamila's Books © 2002 Joanna Carey
Mona © 2001 Jamila Gavin

ISBN 1 4052 0088 X

A CIP catalogue record for this title is available from the British Library.

Printed and bound in Great Britain by Cox and Wyman Ltd, Reading, Berks.

Contents

An interview with
Jamila Gavin
by Joanna Carey

Jamila Gavin lives in Stroud, Gloucestershire. She has two grown up children, both of whom have left home. Her daughter Indi works for a Bristol based charity, Motivation, which organises projects for the design and manufacture of wheelchairs in the developing world. Her son Rohan is a screen writer in Los Angeles. Jamila lives alone now, in a companionable terrace tucked into the foot of a hill, with a garden that rises so steeply that from the end of it – or the top – you can see right over the rooftops to the Laurie Lee country of the Slad Valley beyond. It's a cosy house full of books, paintings and music. While a piano, laden with piles of sheet music, dominates the downstairs area, the writing is all done in an upstairs study, overlooking the garden. 'No, I don't do much gardening,' she says with a smile, 'but I do like to watch it grow . . .'

An interview with

Jamila Gavin

by Joanna Carey

Beginnings

Did you always want to be a writer?

No . . . When I was little, I imagined I would grow up to

be a composer – or, failing that, a spy or an acrobat.

What are your memories of
early childhood?

I was born in India, in the foothills of the Himalayas. I

have only the most gorgeous memories of the first five

to six years of my life – mostly in India, but we did come

back to England now and then.

Family photo, 1942. My mother holds me, surrounded by our Indian family. My brother Philip stands at the centre, hands in pockets.

We were living in Batala, a small town in the Punjab, where my father was given the job of setting up a teacher training college in an abandoned Sikh palace – an elegant building originally built for the son of one of the great rulers of the Punjab, which by this time had fallen into disrepair and which features in my book *The Wheel of Surya*. We lived in the palace for a bit – it was a marvellous place to explore – then when the college was fully operational we moved to a British-built mission bungalow with a veranda.

Although, at this time, the war was going on in Europe, my brother and I were too young to realise what that meant, and life, for us, was idyllic. The food was wonderful – chapattis, mountains of rice, and delicious mangoes to suck. I remember playing all day. We swam, we rode bikes and, what I specially

Me with my brother on one of our trips to England.

loved was riding on the crossbar of my father's bicycle. A lot of the time I was tagging along after my brother – climbing trees and exploring. My brother was sent off to boarding school very young but I didn't go to school in those early years. I was always very close to my mother and she taught me a lot at home.

What were your parents like?

My parents came from very different parts of the world. My mother was from Staffordshire, after graduating from Cambridge she trained as a teacher and, as a way of seeing the world, got a job with the Church Missionary Society teaching in Iran (then Persia). There she met my father, an Indian, who was also a teacher with the CMS, who had arrived there from the opposite direction. When they decided to get married, my mother came back to England to tell her parents and then returned to India. They were married in Bombay.

My father was a Christian with a Christian surname, Phillips, and I was told that many years earlier, my great, great grandfather had saved the life of a British officer during British rule in India. The British officer had converted him to Christianity, and had given him his name. Although he remained a committed Christian, when he was involved in the fight for independence my father changed his name back to the original family name of Khushal-Singh.

My mother was a very intelligent woman. She had

My parents' wedding, in Bombay.

studied literature and philosophy, she taught me elementary French, she introduced me to the piano – she played a lot of Mozart and Schubert – and she read to me. And in the evening, after the heat of the day we would take long walks in the guava groves, through the fields of sugar cane and mustard seed, or in the Muslim cemetery. She was a wonderful storyteller and on those walks she would tell me the story of whatever she happened to be reading at the time – whether it was Charles Dickens, Agatha Christie, Dostoevsky . . . We didn't have any children's books, but there was a wonderful book of ghost stories – an old-fashioned leather bound book that had a lot of old engravings in it. I loved looking at that, long before I could read.

Culturally we were an unusual family, but it was never a problem – both my parents believed in the universal ideals of Christianity and Gandhism – my father was a passionate follower of Gandhi. My brother and I were brought up in the Church of England faith, but we lived happily alongside Hindus, Muslims, Sikhs, and Parsees.

What are your best memories of India?

I suppose my best memories, my happiest memories, are of the outdoor life, the visual, sensual delights of India, sugar cane, the mangoes, shady verandas, mountains. And riding on the crossbar of my father's bike and walking in the evenings with my mother, listening to her playing the piano.

And your worst memories?

My parents didn't always get on too well together. Theirs was a love/hate relationship . . . the loving part was wonderful, but the hate side of it made us all unhappy at times. He was so outgoing and sociable, whereas she was very private. But because of my father's work, they were apart for long stretches of time, which made things easier.

*　*　*

Changing times

What were your first impressions of England?

In 1944, it seemed as though the war was coming to an end and my mother decided to take me and my brother back to England to see her family. Leaving my father back in India we sailed on a P&O Liner, with a convoy of battleships to protect us from the danger of German torpedoes. The sea voyage was wonderful – I would watch the ocean hour after hour, and I loved the huge dining room, the swimming pool and the shops – it really was another world.

But of course when we got to England, the war wasn't over at all. In London there were bombs and doodlebugs and ruins. It was cold, grey and dismal. Even though I was only very young I can remember the sound of the air raid warning, and going into the Anderson shelter. And when we came out, the windows of my aunt's flat were all blown in. Eventually my mother decided to take us back to India, and we travelled to the port on a train with the windows blacked out. There were lots of children on the boat and most of them, including me, got measles.

And what happened next?

Back in India, my mother had a third child – a boy – but there was something wrong with him, and he died. I remember being allowed to see his tiny body and asking why he was blue. I remember my father weeping, and I remember my intense curiosity about the meaning of death – I just couldn't understand how the baby could have stopped being alive. It was a terrible sadness and in addition to that, there was all the unrest and violence in the build up to Independence and partition. We lived right on the border between India and Pakistan – Muslims were crossing from India to Pakistan, Hindus were crossing from Pakistan to India

– there were riots and my mother felt increasingly threatened by the violence.

Leaving my father behind in the thick of it (the palace that had been his college now became a refugee centre), we left for England again. In fact we went back and forth several times, which made schooling rather difficult. In England, we stayed in Ealing, on the outskirts of London, in a flat that belonged to some friends of my mother, and I was slotted in to school there, first at St Saviour's Primary School, and later on at Christchurch Junior.

What do you remember about school at this time?

The first thing I remember about school was the way teachers would prod you with a finger, I didn't like that, but at least it didn't hurt – it wasn't like being whacked. We certainly got whacked at my junior school – for any minor misdemeanour – talking, mucking about,

St. Saviour's, Ealing, 1948.

giggling – by a teacher called Miss Humphries. She must single-handedly have been responsible for an awful lot of school phobia. She not only whacked people on the back of the legs, with a ruler, but also she was so *sarcastic* – she loved to put you down. The sarcasm I think was really worse than the whacking.

But generally, were you happy?

I think happiness is to do with one's inherited capacity for it, and I really do think think I have a happiness gene – I love people, I love friends. And as a child I was happy with my friends, happy galloping

At Trinity College.

round pretending to be on a horse or pretending to be a spy, engaged on some espionage work in London, and happy pretending to be a ballet dancer. I loved painting and music – that's what really gave me happiness – I loved my piano lessons.

Do you remember having a best friend?

My best friend in India was a parsee girl called Maharukh, and in Ealing, when I went to St Saviour's, my best friend was a girl called Doreen. She was blonde and blue-eyed – completely the opposite to me with my dark skin and black hair. She remained a good friend for a long time, though sadly I've lost touch with her now.

Me, Doreen and Doreen's cousin Wendy.

What kind of a life did you lead in London? Was it a very sheltered existence after your wonderful outdoor life in India?

On the contrary! We played outside all the time, in back gardens, on street corners, in the parks. Nobody seemed to worry about us, it seemed perfectly all right for children to have plenty of unsupervised freedom. I suppose one big difference was that in those days not only were there more policemen around, but there were park keepers – figures of authority who gave a sense of security, and who weren't afraid to exercise a bit of discipline in the case of any bad behaviour, so that made it much easier, much safer for younger children like us.

Did you keep any pets at that time?

No, but I was always very vigilant about collecting up stray dogs in the park and taking them to the police station. They weren't always strays, unfortunately.

Did you ever go on holiday, out of London - apart from your trips to India?

There was a farm, near Horsham, that we were sent to, a special place for children whose parents worked for the missionary society. I would go on the Greenline bus, all on my own sometimes, if my brother wasn't coming, and I would stay for two or three weeks. I spent my seventh birthday there whilst my mother was having my sister Romie. And I remember to this day being given a gift of a bow and arrow by one of the boys there. I'm afraid rather rudely I rejected it – I still feel bad about that. The farm was in deep countryside and we went for long walks. I had wonderful holidays there, and I think it was there that I began to discover reading for myself, things like *Milly Molly Mandy* and *Little Grey Rabbit,* and the *Flower Fairies* – I firmly believed in fairies at this stage.

Where were you when India finally gained Independence in 1947?

I was in London, and my father was still working in India. In 1949, he got a new job in Poona, near Bombay and we went back to India to join him, together with my younger sister, who he hadn't yet seen. And there I was sent to a Church of England convent, where the nuns encouraged my musical talent, which is when I began to feel serious about studying music. After that I was moved to an American school in Mussoorie, near where I was born, which I really hated – so I was sent back to the convent before finally, in 1953, we came to England for good.

Do you have any regrets about this rather restless childhood?

Not at all! I found it all intensely exciting and adventurous. I loved it, though I suppose my education suffered – I had no experience of an academic approach to learning. And my maths wasn't too good – in fact I was virtually innumerate and, with all those different schools, I was confused by having to learn pounds, shillings and pence, rupees, annas and paises, and then at the American school, dollars, nickels and dimes.

*　　*　　*

Settling in England

When you came to London, what aspects of English life did you specially enjoy?

One of the great delights of England was the public library in Ealing. The building itself, Walpole House, was very imposing. I think it was designed by Sir John Soane and it had steps up to it, and pillars. There was an oak-floored lobby, with the children's library on the right, and the adults' straight ahead. I loved the whole thing, it gave you a real sense of occasion. I loved the squeak of my rubber soles on the polished floor and the way everyone whispered . . . and it was so satisfying to have your book stamped – kerplonk! And to be given a ticket which you slotted into a little pocket inside the book. I really enjoyed that. I'd collect my books, and then go along to the adults' library to look for my mother.

After so many moves and so much travelling, you must have had a fairly unconventional approach to life ... what was it like starting secondary school in England knowing that you weren't going to be uprooted again? Was it difficult to settle down? What sort of school were you sent to?

I'm afraid I was quite an unruly pupil, and the school my mother chose (the Notting Hill and Ealing High School for Girls) was rather posh. I tended to be somewhat disruptive if I was bored, though there were things I enjoyed enormously, like the choir, the orchestra and the country dancing. And they took my interest in music seriously. It was a wonderful school for art and music.

Did you ever study Indian music?

Alas, no. My training was all in Western music. And much to my sorrow, I never studied Indian dance, either – I've always wanted to, and I think about it every time I go to India. Since growing up, I've learnt to love it more and more.

Are there any teachers you remember in particular?

I was given a place at Trinity College to study music on Saturdays – this was in the days when local authorities funded such things – so that meant I was busy with my music every weekend, which I loved. And I was lucky to have a really life-enhancing, inspirational music teacher called Gladys Puttick. She was passionate about her work – not just a brilliant pianist herself, who could launch off, at the drop of a hat, into any of the Bach Preludes and Fugues, but she was also particularly good at teaching us to play interesting contemporary pieces that sounded a lot more ferocious and difficult than they really were. An unforgettable teacher. She taught me from my early days in the junior department of Trinity College, right through until I was 20.

But after O-levels, I really didn't want to stay on at school and I left at 15. Before going to Trinity College to study piano full time, I spent a year at a boarding school in Switzerland. It was a well-regimented place where I not only improved my French, and studied piano at the Lausanne Conservatoire, but also, in spite of the eagle-eyed principal who strongly disapproved of her girls gadding about on non-academic extra-mural activities, I managed to have an interesting social life. I remember, in particular, some clandestine meetings with a young man – a comte, no less – who was rumoured to be the grandson of one of the former crowned heads of Europe. He drove a splendid white

Mercedes, so there was never any problem about getting back to school in time . . .

*   *   *

Adult life

After music college, what was your first job?

It was after my first year at Trinity College that I had an opportunity to make a radio programme. Just on the off chance, I wrote to the BBC and said

I was travelling to India and would like to make recordings of my experiences there. And to my surprise they agreed and gave me an enormous EMI tape recorder to take with me. It weighed a ton, and I felt

Me aged 18.

so responsible for it, I couldn't let it out of my sight for a moment, so it was rather an encumbrance – but the programme, *Journey to Assam*, was broadcast, both on the Home Service and the World Service. I sounded terribly stilted – like the Queen!

Then I went to work at the BBC, first of all in radio, then TV, in music and arts. I married a BBC producer, and then my children were born and they became a full time job. (My marriage ended in 1989.)

So how did you start writing – was it something you'd had up your sleeve all along?

Well I'd always kept a notebook, and I had always felt that I ought to be able to make use of my Indian experiences, but I couldn't work out exactly how to do it, or even how to formulate an approach. But really what got me writing was when my children started school and began to experience racism. I was obviously aware of the way people regarded me - as someone who was 'half Indian' or 'coloured' and it was odd to hear myself described as 'that Indian

With my daughter, Indi.

woman'. I could laugh at being called a 'Paki hippy' but it was distressing when my children became upset. The school didn't know what to do except reprimand the offending children. I felt I could help by writing stories about characters from different ethnic backgrounds.

And then, in mid-80s Marilyn Malin, a far-sighted publisher who had given me my first opportunity to write, asked for a book about the Asian emigrants to Africa and Britain . . . Memories came flooding back and I had a very powerful image of India, of those fields of mustard seed with that brilliant yellow glow that looks as though the whole place is on fire . . . and suddenly

I realised how I could express all my feelings about my own upbringing. Sadly that project fell through - but now I had a new editor, the remarkable Miriam Hodgson, who was to shape the rest of my writing career, and I began to write *The Wheel of Surya*.

Is music still a large part of your life? Do you play the piano a lot?

Yes I do, I'm usually working on something, and just at this moment I'm getting to grips with a piano duet, 'Ma Vlast' by Smetana. I'm going on a music course in Hungary, and my old college friend Jane and I will be playing this at the opening concert. But I play a lot of other things too – I ramble through Schubert, Beethoven, Bach . . .

At home in The Laurels.

And how do you relax?

Apart from music, I read a lot, I love the theatre, and I adore the cinema. It has always been one of my greatest treats, ever since I was a child. I still remember the thrill of post-war cinema – so glamorous, yet so cheap and accessible for so many people whose lives had been shattered by the war. It was a real escape from misery, from poverty, it offered so much to so many, right across the board – it was a real shared experience. I loved it when I went with my mother all those years ago, and I love it now.

What about sport?

I love skiing – I love the speed.

Are there plans to make feature films from any of your books? How would you feel about that?

Switzerland, 1958.

Well there have been several 'bites' . . . I don't know how I'd feel, seeing my characters taken over by someone else . . . but still, I think if it happens you have to be philosophical about it – just allow it to happen.

Which is your favourite of all the books you've written?

That would have to be the *Surya Trilogy* – simply because I had always felt so strongly that I wanted to write something that would make some sense of so much that has happened in my own life, and that trilogy has given me a sense of fulfilment.

And when you won the Whitbread Award with 'Coram Boy', was that a surprise?

Coram Boy was entirely different from anything else I had done, and I did spend quite a lot of time in a state of semi-terror, wondering if I had bitten off more than I could chew . . . It's not in my nature to feel fully confident about my work, but after the initial responses (particularly that of my editor, Miriam Hodgson), I did have a sneaking feeling that maybe at last I'd written a book that was OK!

And then, when it was shortlisted, I felt it was in with a chance . . . I'd been shortlisted so often before, and when it won, really you know, one of the great pleasures of that was *other people's* delight in my success.

'Coram Boy' was an exceptionally harrowing story - does it still haunt you in any way?

It doesn't exactly haunt me, but whenever I hear on the news about a child being abandoned in a telephone kiosk, or about children in slave ships off the coast of Benin, or in orphanages in Romania, or the dying rooms in China, I can't help thinking that all that has never really gone away. And the characters in that book have become very dear to me.

You say in the foreword to 'Coram Boy' that you have loved those characters almost more than any you have created - which characters in particular were you talking about?

Meshak was very dear to me because he was a such a powerful character, yet so inarticulate. And Aaron, and

Toby – they were so young, so vulnerable, and I suppose I just felt very maternal towards them and several of the other minor characters. And then there was Timothy Parfitt who looked after Aaron when he went to work at Mr Burney's in St Martin's Lane – he's so cheeky, and I love the way he knows his way around London so well, scuttling all over the place, zipping around from Spitalfields to Covent Garden. I enjoyed writing that so much . . .

You are now writing about India again. Have you been back there recently?

I was there earlier this year to launch my books at the Delhi book fair. It will be the first time the books have had an Indian audience . . . I had a very good reaction from the booksellers, but now I'm waiting to see what the children there think of my books.

My new book is set in seventeenth-century Mogul

India, and it's about a Venetian jeweller who gets taken hostage by an Afghan warlord. It starts in Venice, crosses Syria to the Persian Gulf, then reaches the Indian coast and travels on to Agra and the court of Shah Jehan, who would ultimately build the Taj Mahal.

When you are at home, settling down at your desk to write, do you have any special routines? Are there any particular objects without which you cannot work? Are you superstitious in any way?

No, I'm afraid not – I'm rationalist to a fault, to the despair of my friends. I'm surrounded in this part of the country by people who believe in all sorts of weird goings on. I'm always happy to learn about these things, and to enjoy – and to try to understand other people's enthusiasm in these areas, but I just don't believe in alien abductions, crop circles or ghosts. That's not to say that I don't see strange things though, for example, I've had ethereal people wandering through my house and passing through the walls, and I've heard music playing downstairs when there's no one there, but I put that down to 'lucid' dreams, rather than supernatural manifestations. I certainly don't believe in ghosts . . . though, having said that, I did see something strange at Waterloo station not so long ago, under the clock . . . There was this very, very tall man with very piercing blue eyes . . . his coat was billowing up behind him in an odd, floaty way – he looked like an angel, struggling to get his coat on over his wings . . . It was a very striking image . . . Then I looked away for some reason, and when I looked back he was gone! So maybe it was a . . . No! Of course I don't believe in ghosts. Or miracles. And although I won a prize for Bible knowledge when I was six, I'm not religious. I have tried to be, but really, for me, it just doesn't hang together.

When you are writing, do you do a lot of drafting, and redrafting?

Yes I do – and it's so easy with a computer! To be honest, I don't think I'd have made it this far as a writer without a computer – it really has made a huge difference to the way I work.

Originally, when you went to music college to study piano, wasn't it your plan to be a performer? A concert pianist? How do you feel about having become a writer instead? Is it a lonely life?

I think I was quite confused in my late teens. I know that at one point I considered performance, but I really had far too much going on in my life. I was spending too much time studying drama, and having fantasies about theatre, and by the age of 20, although I got a scholarship to Paris, and reached quite a high standard, it wasn't high enough. But when I joined the BBC, working in music and arts, I realised that was where I really wanted to be.

I've still got my music, and now writing has brought me back to so many of the other things I always wanted to do. As well as all the children's books, I've written short stories for the radio, I've done a radio play, I've written stage plays ('Monkey in the Stars') and a musical. I've seen my work adapted for the television and there's always something new on the horizon – I'm currently working on a stage adaptation of the *Just So Stories* for the Polka Theatre. And my books take me travelling all over the place, and I love to travel. So yes, I'm very very happy to be a writer – and, with so much going on, never lonely.

Do you have a clear idea of who your readers are?

No, I haven't a clue. I'm always being taken by surprise

by the variety of people who say they've read my books, children of all ages. Sometimes I meet grown-ups who tell me they read my books when *they* were children – now that really does make me feel my age! And I know that teachers value my books for their multi-ethnic qualities.

When you started writing you were concerned about the levels of racism in this country - has that changed over the years?

There is still plenty of racism, but it has changed its nature, it's more complex and fragmented. There's still a suspicion of 'foreigners', and there's a lot to be done, especially in the field of education, in the way of letting people from different cultures know that they belong, encouraging them to make an input, and recognising all their different qualities. But that of course is by no means confined to this country, and I do really think that, in general, Britain has finally accepted the fact that we *are* a multi-cultural society and people have begun to relish the diversity. That's what, for me, makes it such an exciting place to live and to work. And although as a writer I started out addressing these matters, I now feel none of those constraints, and I love the fact that I'm free to write about anything and everything.

Do you feel pigeon-holed by being known as a writer of multi-cultural books? Or are you able to write freely without being constrained by such a label?

Although when I first began writing, reflecting multi-cultural Britain was my own personal brief, and it is certainly in that area that I found my voice as a writer, I have never felt that my publishers were trying to limit me in any way. Over the years I've produced such books as *The Hideaway* and *The Wormholers*, neither of which had a multi-cultural angle to them – and of course, *Coram Boy*. I don't feel it is an area I will ever abandon, because it is so much part of who I am – and that's the main thing. However, I feel totally free to respond to whatever subjects inspire me – big or small – and that means writing stays both a fun activity, as well as one which is full of challenge and excitement.

Jamila's Books

An overview by Joanna Carey

Just as we all need a sense of our own identity, we all have a basic need to belong somewhere, and to be accepted on equal terms with everyone else, regardless of race, creed or colour.

As the daughter of an Indian father and an English mother, Jamila Gavin grew up belonging to two very different cultures, and she writes about these matters with great insight. Her first book *The Magic Orange Tree* is a collection of stories written for (and about) young children from a wide variety of cultural backgrounds. In fact they are for children everywhere, whether they are from Africa, Asia, Poland, Cyprus or Britain – the one thing all the children have in common in these stories is that they all live in cities. This collection was a remarkable debut. With imaginative ideas flying like thistledown in every direction, children are plucked from everyday urban situations to take starring roles in their own fantasies.

Fantasy and reality

While some writers manage to blur the line between fantasy and reality, here there is no line, and each child has, for a short while, direct access to a liberating world where the impossible can and does happen. A little girl gets carried up in the air by an enormous bird who thinks her glittery party dress would make a fine addition to his nest. Aziz, in a wheelchair, finds himself performing incredible stunts on a huge motorbike. In the title story, Joey lives in an urban street with a small concrete backyard. His parents often talk about their childhood in the Caribbean, a far off place where oranges grow on trees. Then when Joey dreams an orange tree of his own, right there in the backyard, it is so real that the neighbours come round to pick the fruit. 'Oh my, I haven't tasted oranges like this since I was a boy,' says his grandfather. The writing – like the magic – is simple and direct and so, it seems, is the message: everyone's got imagination, why not use it?

Kamla and Kate is another book for younger readers, and the magic Jamila is writing about here is the magic of friendship. Friendship is important in all her books, and the friends here are two little girls alike in almost every way – they go to the same school, live in the same street and laugh at the same jokes – but they come from very different cultures. And when Kate goes go play at

Kamla's house her first reaction is to screw up her nose – 'your house smells funny,' she says – but the fact that Kate doesn't like curry is neither here nor there. It doesn't stop Kate enjoying Kamla's Diwali party, where she learns a little about Indian dancing, and it doesn't stop her trying to persuade Kamla to join her at ballet classes.

Grandpa Chatterji, again for younger readers, is about another Indian family living in England. When Grandpa Chatterji comes to visit from Calcutta, the children are astonished and delighted by his very different outlook on life. Although they've prepared him the best bed in the house, with the softest duvet and the plumpest pillows, Grandpa Chatterji has no need of such things – he prefers to sleep on the floor. He meditates in the garden at the crack of dawn, he does yoga exercises and wears a simple dhoti around the house, putting an apron over it when he takes over the kitchen to do some real Indian cooking. Warm, witty and wonderfully entertaining, this was the first of Jamila's books to be adapted for television.

Indian legends

Jamila has made several retellings of Indian legends. *Three Indian Princesses* tells the stories of Savitri, Damayanti and Sita, taken from ancient sources like the 3000-year-old *Mahabharata* and the *Ramayana*, an epic poem from the second century BC. These are sumptuous stories, featuring thundering chariots, richly caparisoned elephants, golden swans and mighty rajahs – stories which, beautifully written, give us a real taste of the original splendour, and which clearly fuelled Jamila's imagination when she came to write the *Surya* trilogy year later. There's Savitri, for example, who lived in a 'magnificent palace, with large beautiful rooms to explore, and cool courtyards with fountains in which to rest . . . Savitri could see the jungle from her balcony . . . she loved to watch the green parrots burst upwards from the pink dawn sky, and swoop around the palace . . . she loved to catch a glimpse of the spotted deer as they sprang through the dappled shadows; or the grey mongoose spinning and curling down the old gnarled trunks of the trees. Sometimes she saw a small solemn boy herding dusty buffalo down to the river.' And, if you've read *The Wheel of Surya*, it's tempting to think that the small boy might be Jaspal, in a previous incarnation.

Identity and cultural differences

There's a very clear line of development in Jamila's writing. Before she began the trilogy,

Jamila wrote *The Singing Bowls* and this is where she begins to explore in depth the matter of identity and cultural differences. Ronnie is a half English, half Indian teenage boy in the throes of an identity crisis sparked off by the death of his very elderly grandfather. In the far off days when India was the 'jewel in the Crown of the British Empire', Ronnie's grandfather had been Assistant District Commissioner of the Durgapur District, in the United Province. Under strange and dramatic circumstances he had adopted and brought back to England an Indian baby boy. This child was to become Ronnie's father . . . Although he has always known that his father was Indian, Ronnie has been brought up to feel *'completely English in thought, word and deed. His Indian blood had been deemed at best, exotic, explaining his olive skin, straight black hair and dark brooding eyes, and at worst something best not talked about. Especially after his father mysteriously disappeared.'* Ronnie's mother is strangely unsympathetic about Ronnie's curiosity, and sees the Indian connection as almost irrelevant. *'Your father wasn't Indian,'* she says, *'except by race. He was as English as you or me. He never knew India.'*

But when Ronnie learns more about his father's background he sets off on a journey to India to unravel the whole story. With an illuminating historical background and a strong mystical element (to which the above mythological retellings offer considerable insight), this is an exciting, many layered story which, like an early black and white movie, magically comes flickering to life as Ronnie goes through a bundle of old family letters – and then hurtles into full colour, wide-screen bustling reality when he arrives in India on his obsessive search for the truth. It's clear, even in this early book, that

Jamila has what every writer must have, which is real love for her young characters however difficult they may be, and, equally important, she loves them enough to let them grow up. Laced with riveting details of train journeys, street children, and the harsher realities of life in India, along with a powerful spiritual dimension, the writing of *The Singing Bowls* has a restless intensity that shows the author working her way towards the astonishing breadth and complexity of the *Surya* trilogy, the first volume of which was published three years later.

The 'Surya' trilogy

The Wheel Of Surya is set in India, in a village in the Punjab. War is about to break out in Europe, and in India, prior to independence, partition and the creation of Pakistan, political unrest and violence is causing fear and anxiety amongst the British community there. In an early scene, Miss Alcott, a bossy woman who is the sister of the Church of England vicar, gives a little advice to Dora Chadwick, the wife of a local English schoolmaster.

'You don't want your child getting too familiar with the natives. It can lead to problems later on. I've seen it happen. People must know their place in life, and if you don't mind my saying, I believe it's idealists like you, with a misguided desire to promote equality, who have helped to fuel these disgraceful aspirations among the Indians. Independence my foot. How can they rule themselves, I mean look at them. The vast majority haven't progressed since the invention of the wheel.'

Dora already feels uneasy about her position as a British *memsahib*, and her husband Harold Chadwick, a liberal and an idealist, is of the opinion that the Indians *'were one of the most civilised and cultured people on earth at a time when we Britons were running around in woad.'* And it is Harold who, as a teacher, encourages the young man Govind not only to go to university, but also to travel to England for further study, leaving his young wife Jhoti behind. Jhoti is then employed by the Chadwicks to help with their children. Jhoti (who was only 13 when she married Govind), has two children herself, Marvinder and Jaspal, and soon, in spite of the vast cultural gap between them the lives of the two families are inexorably entwined.

Within the necessary constraints of its historical context, with real events and real figures like Ghandi and Nehru in the background, Jamila Gavin is a bold and generous storyteller. And she writes with a cinematic breadth to describe the countryside, the sounds, the smells, the heat, the vivid intensity of the colour, and the romance of the deserted palace where the children play. In a swift series of flashbacks she explains the implications of the political situation, the conflict between the different religions and, as in Jhoti's case, the bewildering experiences of a child bride. She's always ready to zoom in on the smallest details – details which, however serendipitous they may seem, often have a subtle significance, as in the scene at the beginning where two little Indian children are fighting for possession of an empty tin – not just any old tin, but a Bournville chocolate tin which has been retrieved from the English schoolmaster's rubbish tip.

Jamila writes revealingly about the very different expectations the Indian and the British parents have of their children – while Marvinder sorts rice and washes dishes, and Jaspal herds the buffalo, Edith has an *ayah* to dress her and to brush her golden hair. The intriguing dynamics of the friendship that grows between the two girls are subtly noted – as are the relationships between siblings in each family: in the Chadwick household, the following scene shockingly reveals Edith's feelings towards her baby brother and sister:

> It came from under the toy cupboard, the snake. Edith saw its eyes first of all, like bright beads, glinting in the dusty darkness. Then as it ventured further into the room, its head swayed from side to side, like a scout examining the lie of the land. Every now and then its tongue flashed from its mouth like lighting.
>
> The lizard on the wall froze, still as an ornament, and even the sunlight, falling in warm dappled patches across the carpet, seemed cool.

Edith watched it from her rocking horse. She only paused for a moment with surprise, her mouth opening instinctively to exclaim, but shutting it again without a sound.

The playpen stood in the middle of the carpet. Jhoti had just bathed and changed the twins . . . Ralph saw it first; chortled with delight at the undulating patterns on its scaly back; reached a hand through the wooden bars of the playpen, longing to grasp its writhing body. Edith went on rocking. She didn't say a word, though her eye was fixed on the snake.

At the sight of Ralph's hand, the creature halted. It lifted its narrow head, its tongue flickering with curiosity . . . Edith stopped rocking a second time . . . the room, the lizard, the older sister stopped breathing. How long is a moment? Then, somewhere in the universe, a god blinked and life started again. The snake moved on, sliding away towards the watery coolness of the bathroom. Ralph withdrew his hand, disappointed, and Edith went on rocking.

It's the things left unsaid in this passage that make it so eloquently unnerving. The skill here is that of a film maker, creating, frame by frame, an unforgettable atmosphere. When a subsequent tragedy causes the death of the two babies, the story moves on under a veil of sadness and guilt from which no one is entirely free.

In the escalating violence and bloodshed surrounding the fight for independence, Jaspal and Marvinder, separated from their mother, decide to travel to England to find their father. They undertake an epic journey, across a scarred, scorched country amid fire, famine and massacre. With creaking bullock carts transporting thousands of refugees this way and that in search of a homeland, there's powerful imagery that can take you back to stories of classical mythology, or fast forward you to TV news reports from so many parts of the world today.

The sea voyage that takes the children to England offers a welcome period of respite, with brisk and efficient adults in charge at last. And, with talk of porridge, garters and haircuts, there's a pervading sense of the country that awaits them. But of course after the extravagant excesses of their Indian experience, England is bleak, war-torn and monochromatic. And their father, when they find him, is far from being the heroic warrior/scholar that they have imagined him to be. In spite of all that's gone before, their reunion is really only the beginning of this absorbing trilogy.

With its vast historical sweep, its urgent narrative thrust, and its complex structure, the scale on which this story has been created is astonishing. From the outside, it may seem hard to see how this could be a children's book, but like all the best books for children it works at many levels of understanding. Importantly (as in *The Singing Bowls*), it's the children who initiate most of the action, in many cases because of the negative qualities of some of the adults, many of whom are flawed characters, or characters brought down by circumstances beyond their control . . . There's Dora Chadwick, consumed by grief, her husband wracked with guilt. Govind, though clever, is ineffective and impulsive, easily swayed. Jhoti though, in spite of her lack of education, has spiritual strength. So it is Jaspal, proud and fiercely independent, and Marvinder, sensitive, intelligent and musically gifted, who drive the story. And, interwoven with elements of mysticism, spirituality and morality, it has the timeless, redemptive quality of a fairy tale.

'Coram Boy'

After a number of books for younger readers,

Jamila took a dramatically different turn with *Coram Boy*. The winner of the 2001 Whitbread Award, it's a bold, unusual novel with a challenging theme that few authors would dare to approach, but, as with the *Surya* trilogy, she handles it with grace and authority.

Set in Gloucestershire and London in the eighteenth century, *Coram Boy* tells the story of a hideous trade in unwanted children. In 1741 Thomas Coram founded a charitable organisation that took in unwanted children, and undertook to give them a good upbringing and education. But there were vast numbers of unwanted children and, cashing in on the good name of the charity, certain villainous characters travelled around masquerading as 'Coram men'. For an agreed sum they would take unwanted babies and children, promising to deliver them to the foundling hospital, but in fact, having pocketed the money, they would either sell them on as slave labour, or simply 'dispose' of them. As Jamila Gavin says in her foreword, 'the high-ways and by-ways of England were littered with the bones of little children'. And it wasn't just poor, uneducated people who availed themselves of the services of the Coram man – hypocrisy and double standards were rife in this society. And around these horrific facts she has woven a story of operatic dimensions, that pits the elements of greed, cruelty, hypocrisy against those of innocence, love, friendship. The story centres round two boys, one saved from an African slave ship, the other the illegitimate son of an aristocratic young man who turned his back on his family fortune to follow a career in music. Friendship and music are major themes in Jamila's work, and here they work overtime to rise above the cruel realities upon which this novel is based. Much of the action takes place in a choir school and together with a historically authenticated performance of the *Messiah* at the Coram hospital, with a cameo role for Handel himself, the singing provides a vital escape valve for the emotional intensity. There's a scene of extraordinary magic when Meshak, the simpleton son of the villainous 'Coram man', hears the 'piercing sweetness' of the music coming from the cottage in the woods – a creation which itself resonates with fairy tale symbolism. And it's with a touch of genius that Meshak is introduced – an unknown dimension, a primitive figure, a holy fool, an idiot savant, an innocent abroad – he's all these things, an ungainly simpleton with the physical charm of a gargoyle, and the social skills of a peeping Tom. But Meshak has a big heart and a childlike capacity for undying love which, together with the initiative of the two boys, changes the whole course of the story.

Words and music

Music has always been an important part of Jamila's life, and her work. It's probably because she's a musician herself that she can make reference to music without sounding false, or over-researched and she can use it as a subtle, natural means of expression. While music is uplifting, it's also a great leveller. This fact is especially evident in the *Surya* trilogy – right at the beginning there is the sound of Mozart coming 'like a strange spirit bird' from the mission bungalow as the English sahib and his memsahib make their nightly music, awakening the interest and capturing the imagination of Marvinder and her mother. There's a bizarre scene where Marvinder takes over from the rheumaticky old Ram Singh at the back of the British church pumping the organ, while the organist thunders out hymns for the British congregation. And, with yet another sly angle on the insularity of the British community, there's a reference to a Gilbert and Sullivan performance by the local Women's Institute . . .

Then, in post-war England there is the sound of the Jewish refugee, Dr Silberman playing Bach on his violin in the basement, and there's Jaspal, hiding out from his racist tormentors in the cellar of a bombed-out house in Clapham where he finds an old wind-up gramophone, and listens to a Palm Court orchestra and a melancholy rendition of 'Have You Ever Been Lonely? Have You Ever Been Blue?' And there's a telling scene in *The Eye of the Horse*, where Marvinder, now a talented violinist, takes part in a music festival in London:

'I award Marvinder Singh the highest mark of the section, ninety per cent,' the adjudicator said. There was a gasp, and everyone looked round and then burst into applause.

'It's amazing that you seem to understand our music so well,' commented the kindly adjudicator, when she went up to get her certificate.

'Thank you,' murmured Marvinder, wondering what on earth she meant by 'our music'.

That incident was set in the 1950s – attitudes have changed now. The world has changed, but Jamila Gavin's books, in all their subtle variety, continue to illuminate the fact that, whoever we are, wherever we're from, we're all in it together.

Bibliography
In date order

The Magic Orange Tree

Methuen 1979

The children in these stories live in the same city, but in their dreams they can go anywhere and anything might

happen. They can have adventures on moonlit nights, fly through the air on the backs of dragons or be whisked away by giants birds . . .

Three Indian Princesses

Methuen 1987

Jamila's retelling of three Hindu tales. Savitri and
Satyvan begin their marriages
together, but the stars tell of
Satyvan's death in just one
year. Princess Damayanti is
loved by all – but the demon
Kali wants her for himself . . .

The Singing Bowls

Methuen 1989

Teenager Ronnie Saville hears a strange story from his
dying grandfather, about his own father's adoption from
the daughter of a holy man in India. Intrigued, Ronnie
travels to India, taking with him his father's sacred
singing bowls . . .

Grandpa Chatterji

Methuen 1993

Neeta and Sanjay's grandfather, Grandpa Chatterji, comes to visit them and they discover what a loving and surprising grandpa he is . . .

The Surya Trilogy

I   The Wheel of Surya

Methuen 1992

Fleeing from their burnt-out village as civil war rages in the Punjab, Marvinder and Jaspal are separated from their mother, Jhoti. Escaping across India, they face a daily fight for survival. Their only hope is to reach England, and the father they barely know . . .

II The Eye of the Horse

Methuen 1994

Jaspal and Marvinder's father, Govind Singh, is in

prison in England. Jaspal longs to return to his village in the Punjab, but Marvinder has found friends, and a gift as a violinist. But she too feels drawn towards India . . .

III The Track of the Wind

Mammoth 1997

The Singh family is reunited in India, but Jaspal feels he must leave to fight for Sikh independence. Marvinder yearns for Patrick O'Grady, but must enter an arranged marriage nonetheless. How can Jhoti find happiness for her husband and her children?

Grandpa's Indian Summer

Mammoth 1996

Neeta and Sanjay go to visit Grandpa Chatterji this time, in his home in Calcutta.

The Wormholers

Mammoth 1996

Natalie, Chad and Sophie find themselves lost down a wormhole. Through the fabric of reality they enter a whole new universe. As wormholers, they can exist on all planes at once, wherever they feel comfortable. It seems perfect – but is it a trap?

The Monkey in the Stars

Mammoth 1998

Hanuman the Monkey God appears in Amrita's bedroom to take her on a magical journey into the story of Diwali, the Festival of Light. Amrita sees brave Prince Rama and his brother tricked by demons. She sees the beautiful Princess Sita kidnapped by Ravana, Lord of the Demons. And she witnesses the final battle, when good fights evil to bring light into the world.

Coram Boy

Egmont 2000

In eighteenth century England, Coram men offered to

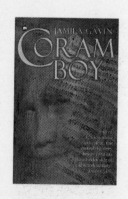

take unwanted children to Thomas Coram's new foundling hospital, but many merely buried their charges by the roadside. The illegitimate son of an heir to a great estate and an African boy rescued from a slave ship find themselves battling for their lives in a story of love, music, cold aristocrats and warm friendship.

Fine Feathered Friend

Egmont 2001

Raju is thrilled by the bustle of his home in Bombay, and dreads spending the summer on his uncle's farm. But Raju soon finds that in its own quiet way, country life is captivating too . . .

Three Indian Goddesses

Egmont 2001

These contemporary stories were inspired by Hindu tales. Shanta is chosen to dance at the temple by the sea, but Kali has put a terrible curse on the place. Amrita flies with Hanuman into the story of Diwali. And there's a lot more to Anil and Kiki's cousin Durga than meets the eye . . .

Danger by Moonlight

Egmont 2002

Filippo has never seen his father. Before Filippo was born, Father left their home in Venice to travel to the land of Hindustan to work for the Emperor Shah Jehan. He never came back. After twelve years, a mysterious stranger brings a message from a far off land . . .

Out of India

Hodder Children's Books 2002

Jamila's account of her early childhood in India and the endless questions her schoolmates in England used to ask about her native country.

Celebration Stories: Coming Home

Hodder Wayland 2002

Preeta and her family have lots to do for Divali. They go

out shopping for new clothes for the celebration, but Preeta gets lost in the crowd. As Prince Rama and Princess Sita's story begins, will Preeta reach home in time for the party?

Mona

Jamila Gavin

'Meet Mona!'

Uncle Cedric stood in the doorway holding a leash. The light from the hallway fell on him, but it trailed away into darkness behind him, so they couldn't quite see what was on the end of the leash.

'Oh great! It's a dog!' cried Duane, who had always wanted a dog.

'Bags I walk him,' shouted Saffron, as usual trying to be the first to stake a claim.

'Her,' corrected Uncle Cedric.

The children rushed outside excitedly. But when they saw what was on the end of the lead, they stopped short. Duane backed away uncertainly till he reached his mother's side. Saffron just stood there staring, dumbstruck for once. Molotov, their cat, looked electrified and fled.

'Well, you'd better come in,' said Mum. She was still feeling half cross because she had let Uncle Cedric twist her arm and agreed to look after his pet for a week while he went away. She realised he hadn't told her what kind of pet, but Uncle Cedric had always had dogs, so she assumed it was a dog.

Being a very house-proud sort of a mum, she didn't care for dogs. They left hair everywhere and a strong smell – especially after a walk in the rain. She was a cat person. But Uncle Cedric had always been so generous with them in the past, she felt she couldn't refuse.

'I can't stop,' said Uncle Cedric. 'My car's on a yellow line, and in any case, I'm a bit on the late side. Look, here's everything you need.' He thrust a large holdall into the hallway. 'It's got her feeding bowl, pet food, you know biscuits, cereal and things – but, really, she eats anything except meat. She's vegetarian. Otherwise, give her your leftovers. Whatever. Oh – and I've put in a whole bag of mini Mars Bars. She's very partial to those. You can make her do anything with a Mars Bar.'

'Uncle,' said Saffron strangely. 'What kind of dog is that?' She peered into the gloom.

Uncle Cedric tugged the lead. Something black moved within the darkness. It came blinking into the light. 'Her name's Mona,' said Uncle Cedric. 'You know – after Mona Lisa. She's beautiful isn't she?'

She had large, flappy ears with pinky grey insides; she had a funny thin straight tail which fluffed out at the end, and four little cloven feet – only little – because they supported a great round belly which hung beneath a huge, shining, black, silky body. She gazed up at them with small squidgy eyes and a snuffling snout.

'She's a PIG!' yelled Mum, backing away, with Duane clinging to her skirts. 'I'm not having a pig in this house. You said it was a dog.'

'I never said it was a dog,' protested Uncle Cedric. 'Anyway, she's as good as a dog – better. She's called a Vietnamese pot-bellied pig.'

'I don't care what she's called, she's a PIG!' insisted Mum.

'I didn't know there were black pigs, only pink pigs,' said Duane.

'This one's from Vietnam. They have black pigs there – they are very intelligent – probably more intelligent than you.'

'I thought pigs only lived on farms,' mumbled Saffron.

'Makes no difference,' retorted Uncle Cedric. 'She's a household pet. She can live anywhere.'

'She's huge,' Mum's voice rose in hopeless protest.

'But she's still loveable. Now look, I'm late – I'll miss my flight. I really must get on. There's nothing for you to do but feed her and take her for walks. Just treat her as if she were a dog. She's house-trained and she doesn't leave hairs all over the place. It's only for a week.' Uncle Cedric thrust the lead into Mum's hands. He dashed back to the car and returned carrying a large dog basket with a blanket. 'She can sleep in this.' He strode past them carrying everything into the kitchen and dumped it in a corner near the fridge. He knelt down in front of his pet, put his arms round her thick body and pressed his nose to her snout. 'Goodbye, Mona my sweetheart,' he drooled. 'See you in a week.' Then he fled.

'CEDRIC!' bellowed Mum.

'Don't forget the Mars Bars!' His voice yelled above the car engine, as he pulled away with a cheery wave.

They stood in the kitchen staring at Mona. Mona stared back.

'Who's Mona Lisa?' asked Duane.

'She's a painting,' muttered Mum. 'A painting of a beautiful woman with a mysterious smile.'

'Oh.'

They looked again at Mona. 'I can't see a mysterious smile,' said Saffron.

The lead had trailed out of Mum's hands. Mona began to shuffle round the kitchen sniffing. Her snout was like a checkout machine, sliding over every object she could reach. When she got to the cupboard below the worktop, she eased her snout under the handle and just opened it.

'Oh no you don't!' cried Mum, leaping forward and grabbing the lead. 'Let's get her food out. She's probably hungry.'

They got out the bowls; one for the cereal and the other for water. They placed them side by side near the kitchen door. Mona *was* hungry. She stuck her snout into the bowl and swoosh, it was gone in one suck. She looked round for more and saw the cat's bowl. Molotov always knew when he'd had enough, and left what he didn't want. Mona stuck her snout into his bowl and swoosh! it was gone.

'Oh, she's one of those,' said Mum wearily. 'An eating machine. Well let's get her to bed.' She fixed her eye on Mona and pointed to the dog basket. 'Bed,' she commanded.

Mona rudely ignored her.

Mum grabbed her collar and tried to pull her over. 'Bed, Mona!' she repeated.

But though all three of them heaved against her, Mona didn't budge an inch.

'Uncle Cedric said she'd do anything for a Mars Bar,' said Duane digging his hand into the holdall for a Mars Bar. He ripped off the wrapper and held it over the basket. 'Here, Mona! Mars Bar!'

Mona turned like a guided missile and was in the basket in a flash.

'Good girl, Mona!' cheered Duane, daring to give her a pat.

Mona flopped an ear over an eye and looked coy.

'Where's Molotov?' Everyone looked around for the cat.

'He'll come when he's ready,' Mum reassured the children. 'He can take care of himself.'

'See you in the morning,' Mum gave Mona a reluctant smile. She switched out the kitchen light, firmly shut the door, and they all trooped up to bed.

The next morning. The next morning. The next . . .

It was like all hell had broken loose – yet silently – for no one heard a thing. Mum went down first as usual. She entered the kitchen and screamed; one great long terrible scream. Saffron and Duane rushed down.

Everything had been tipped out of the fridge; everything had been tipped out of every single cupboard in the kitchen – even the upper cupboards. In the middle of the mayhem, with butter paper licked clean, and jam slurping out of jam-pots, and remains of eggshells, cartons, tins, vegetables and fruit, stood Mona, with her snout in a yogurt pot. She looked up at them and seemed to smile – a mysterious smile.

Mum found wings, flying around between Mona, who she managed to drag outside with the aid of a Mars Bar and tied to the apple tree, and rushing back to clear up the mess, make breakfast, yell at the kids to get ready for school and look for Molotov, who wouldn't be found.

They ate their breakfast standing up, then Mum firmly shut all the cupboards and drawers. She propped a chair in front of the fridge and pushed the kitchen table as a barricade for the kitchen cupboards. Mona was brought in from the garden. 'Basket!' commanded Mum. Mona looked the other way.

'Mars Bar!' yelled the children throwing one into the basket, and Mona went in most obediently.

'Right, let's go!' cried Mum and slammed shut the door.

Mum was waiting for Saffron and Duane when school was over. They walked home. 'We'd better take

Mona to the park,' said Mum. 'She's been in all day.'

Molotov was sitting on the doorstep when they arrived at the gate. He looked miffed, and didn't come down the path to greet them as usual. 'Poor Molotov. He doesn't like having Mona around.'

Inside, they stood before the kitchen door. 'It's funny to think there's a huge black, Vietnamese pot-bellied pig on the other side of that door,' whispered Duane. Mum opened the door. 'Hello Mona, we're ho . . . AAAAAaaaaaH!'

Havoc. The chair in front of the fridge was tipped over and the fridge door was swinging open; all the cupboard doors were open top and bottom and, strewn across the floor, were the chewed, spewed, crunched, scrunched, ripped, stripped and gnawed remains of any tin, jar, carton or bag which had contained anything which could be eaten.

Where was Mona? They heard a deep snore. They didn't see her at first. She had gripped the end of the blanket in her teeth and pulled it right up over her head. But there she was in her basket sound asleep, looking as if she had slept through the mayhem rather than caused it.

'How did she do it?' gasped Saffron looking around aghast.

Mona Lisa's head appeared from under the blanket. She opened an eye, showed her teeth and smiled a mysterious smile.

'Get her out of my sight, or there'll be bacon for breakfast,' yelled Mum.

So while Mum cleared up yet again, Saffron and Duane stuffed their pockets with Mars Bars and took Mona to the park. It took two of them to hold her. She was very strong. But she was as good as gold – so long as a Mars Bar was waved in front of her nose. She stopped at the zebra crossing, she didn't tug and try to chase the little Jack Russell who dashed up yapping and sniffing, and she didn't puncture the football which rolled up to her snout.

Quite a crowd gathered. Not many people take pigs for walks. 'My he's a grand fellow,' said one.

'She,' corrected Saffron.

'What's her name?' asked another.

'Mona. You know, after Mona Lisa,' announced Duane.

'Oh yeah! The lady with the smile.'

That night Mum said to Mona. 'It's the garden shed for you tonight, madam.'

'But Mum . . .' pleaded Saffron. 'She was ever so good in the park. Give her another chance. It'll be cold in the shed.'

Mum was adamant. Firmly, she led Mona up the garden to the wooden shed. Saffron and Duane followed in procession, carrying her basket and bowls. 'There's no food to be found here, madam,' she said icily. 'You'll just have to make do with what's in your bowl.'

Saffron and Duane moaned, 'Poor Mona.' But Molotov looked pleased, and slept in the kitchen that night.

Saffron had now decided she loved Mona, so she was the first to wake up the next morning. Her first thought was Mona. 'Fancy sleeping in that cold shed all night.' She ran downstairs and out into the garden. It was early. Only a few birds cheeped sleepily. The curtains were still drawn in all the surrounding houses. She got to the shed. The door was half open. The garden hose trailed out of it and disappeared across the lawn. Had Mum come out to water the garden early before work?

'Mona?' whispered Saffron, peering inside.

As the daylight flooded in, she saw the terrible sight. Mona had had a feast. She had chewed all the gumboots, ripped up the gardening gloves, mangled the straw hats, gnawed at the tool handles, spilled all the trays of seedlings, knocked over every jar, tin, bottle and, as for the garden hose . . . what had she done with the garden hose? Saffron followed it. It coiled round the apple tree, across the lawn, through a large hole in the fence (the day before it had just been a crack) into next door's garden, across a flattened flower bed, a tipped over bird table, all the way to the treasured vegetable patch of Mrs O'Connor. There lay Mona in a tangle, with the hose wrapped round her neck and legs, looking like a captured battleship. A half-chewed cabbage hung out of her mouth.

'Mona!' gulped Saffron. 'Oh Mona!'

Mona looked up at Saffron innocently and – well – just smiled a mysterious smile.

'This is war,' declared Mum.

She led Mona to the garage. She found a long chain and a padlock. She looped the chain through Mona's dog collar and attached it to a hook on the concrete wall, winding it round and round several times.

Mum took the children to school, and then went on to her job.

At the end of the day, when they all got back, Molotov came purring down the path to greet them. They went to the garage to see Mona.

Mona was sitting in her basket. The chain was still round her neck and still attached to the hook on the wall. No mayhem, no mess, everything was as they left it – except, 'I think she likes eating nuts and bolts,' murmured Duane who noticed a glittering store of them in her basket.

But Mum grinned with satisfaction. 'I think I'm winning,' she said.

'Good girl, Mona!' shouted Saffron throwing her arms round the pig.

That night, after walking Mona in the park, Mum eased the car into the garage and left the pig chained again to the wall for the night. 'This is obviously the best place for her,' she said triumphantly.

'Goodnight Mona!' sighed Saffron, giving her a kiss. 'Be good.'

'Here's some Mars Bars for you,' soothed Saffron, dropping them in the basket.

It was the first morning it had been peaceful since Mona arrived. The kitchen was clean and immaculate when they all trooped down for breakfast; the garden was calm, and when Mum looked out and saw Molotov lazily prowling through the bushes, she knew all was right with the world. They had a leisurely breakfast, and then went to the garage to get the car and check on Mona.

The garage door was closed when Mum went over, but – not locked. Odd. Moments later she was rushing back in distress. The car was gone. So was Mona.

'What's up, Mum?' cried Saffron and Duane.

Mum was on the telephone. 'Police? My car! It's been stolen! And the pig . . .'

'A PIG?' repeated the police woman on the other end.

'Yes . . . no . . . I don't know! But she's gone too. The

car is blue and six years old, registration J 296 F. The pig? She's a black – yes BLACK – a Vietnamese pot-bellied pig. She's called Mona, yes M-O-N-A, you know after Mona Lisa . . .'

The thief thought he was so clever. How silently he had broken into the garage. Easy peasy. People hardly ever locked their cars when they were in the garage. Cor! This one hadn't even shut the passenger door at the back. He closed it gently, and kicked in a chain which was hanging from the front. His torch flashed in the darkness as he opened the driver's door and released the handbrake. He would ease the car out into the road before starting it up.

Soon, he was off, speeding away through the empty neighbourhood heading for the country. He left the city streets behind with their harsh orange lights and roaming police cars. He hit the motorway and sighed with relief.

'A bit of energy, that's what I need,' he murmured tearing off the wrapper of a Mars Bar . . . It was then he glanced in his rear mirror. A face loomed from the back. A black face, with great floppy ears, a nose more like a snout and two beady little eyes which gleamed like a demon. It smiled – a mysterious smile.

Later that day, the phone range. It was the police. 'We've found your car, and your pig – and we caught the thief. At least the pig did. We found the thief blubbing his eyes out with terror, jammed in the car with the horn going, and this ruddy great pig sitting in his lap like a ten ton truck. The thief said he only wanted to eat a Mars Bar and this thing came over the back like a bat out of hell – or rather a pig out of hell. Clever pig, that one. Could do with him in the force.'

'Her,' muttered Mum weakly.

'You can come and get her and the car any time

you like.'

Mum, Saffron and Duane went over to the police station. The car was outside. 'Where's Mona?' asked Mum.

'She's in the cells,' said the policeman. 'Didn't know where else to put her. Took four of us to rugby tackle her to get her in mind you.'

Mum looked at him with pleading eyes. 'You couldn't just keep her there? Could you? Just for three more days?'

'This is a police station not a farm, madam,' replied the policeman sternly.

'Yes. Oh well. It was just a thought,' said Mum wearily. 'I think we're going to need some more Mars Bars, I'm down to the last!'

They went down to the cells. The policeman got out his big bunch of keys and opened the cell door.

Mum waved her last Mars Bar.

'Come on out, Mona Lisa. You're free to go,' said

the policeman.

Mona looked up and smiled.

Other authors in the series

An interview with

Anne Fine

the award-winning author
and Children's Laureate

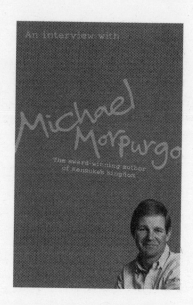

An interview with

Michael Morpurgo

The award-winning author
of Kensuke's Kingdom

An interview with

J. K. Rowling

Creator of the best-selling
Harry Potter

An interview with

Jacqueline Wilson

The best-selling author
of The Illustrated Mum